Everything You Need to Know About

PSYCHIC ATTACKS

Prevention, Symptoms, Solutions and more

Ashwita Goel

Copyright

Reiki is not a replacement for medical assistance. Always seek professional medical support if you experience anything that requires it. Seek the services of a competent professional if expert assistance is required.

To fully understand and to be able to apply the techniques described in this book, the reader should already be introduced to the healing magic of Reiki.

Table of Contents

Preface

I learned Reiki as a teenager along with my mother and sister, prior to which I had already been meditating for many years. And now nearly twenty years later, I'm writing a book I never thought I would – on psychic attacks.

I am not fond of focusing on the negative, in fact I was almost afraid of it. To anyone who starts accessing beings from other realms, things can seem scary in the beginning, especially if the energies one is interacting with are from the lower realms. Even so, I don't think I would have ever thought about writing a book on it.

But how things have changed.

Some years ago as I browsed an interesting website, I read that nearly everyone was carrying at least one entity. At the time I thought they were entirely crazy to believe something like that and dismissed the idea immediately. But now, having worked with so many people and having observed the energy of so many more, I know that they're probably right. It is so prevalent today that mood swings are seen as a normal part of life.

It was an incident recently that prompted me to write about this subject. A beautiful woman who had learned Reiki with me, called in panic. She mentioned that while her life had changed quite drastically over the one week since she learned Reiki, something had suddenly changed. The previous night she had partied with her friends and got drunk, and ever since she was hearing sounds around her room and having thoughts she had never had before.

I wish I could say this is a very rare occurrence. I can say though, that this experience is more common with people who have a spiritual practice – Reiki in her case, but could be anything else. This is not because people on a spiritual pathway get attacked more. It is because when one maintains oneself at a higher vibration, these things become obvious very quickly. Without a strong spiritual practice, an entity could exist for decades, feeding off of a person's energy field and the person would be none the wiser. With a spiritual practice, there's trouble, and then there are solutions. It's not very pleasant, but it is an essential step in facilitating blissful living.

As Reiki is my primary mode of healing, I mention it at various points in the book. This is not to indicate that Reiki is the only means of achieving the goal being talked about, and may be substituted with any other method of healing that you are comfortable with.

Introduction

The unknown instils fear. A term like 'psychic attack' unfortunately triggers much fear among many, which is a pity because fear only enhances the grip it has on you. If we knew nothing about viruses, they would seem just as scary – imagine being told *'there are tiny organisms that you cannot see which insert their own genetic information into your cells and take over the cell's functions, proceeding to then breed billions of other viruses in your body.'* Sounds scary, right? The objective of this book therefore, is not to create fear but to dispel it through awareness.

Just like we think of physical disease as something created by foreign particles, psychic attack is simply when the same thing happens energetically. These energetic parasites take over the body and use it to feed their own desires and obsessions. Unlike physical disease, these attacks may not always be detected and can affect a person for many years before they realize what was going on. That most people don't believe in such a thing doesn't help the cause either.

Psychic attacks have today reached epidemic proportions. Much like browsing through WebMD can leave one feeling like one has a dozen diseases, reading about these topics can sometimes leave a person mistaking ordinary problems as psychic interference, and one must bear this in mind. Such a mistake will prevent a person from doing what is actually needed to fix the problem and prolong the suffering or even make it worse. However, being informed is also extremely important so that one is aware when help needs to be sought.

Is this Even Real?

Much of the information about psychic attacks sounds

way out-there, almost straight out of a horror movie or some fantasy novel. There are many sceptics who believe this to be merely superstition and the result of a weak mind. Personally, I used to think of such people as schizophrenic, even.

The idea of something invisible that can think for itself and harm people is quite scary for most, and most people cope by just pretending it is all fantasy. Those with an affinity towards science also have a tendency to indulge in intellectual snobbery, labelling as a delusion anything that doesn't fit into the current scientific understanding of the universe. Interestingly, it is only an open mind that is truly scientific – one cannot dismiss an idea without first investigating it.

The unfortunate abundance of psychic charlatans and tricksters exploiting weak and disturbed individuals doesn't help this cause any. The media is rife with news about how so many doctors take bribes from pharmaceutical companies and prescribe medicines and surgeries that aren't at all required. This does not mean that medical science is a farce or that all doctors are cheats. In the same way, just because there is a large number of people fooling naïve clients, it doesn't mean that psychic attacks don't exist at all and that all healers are charlatans.

One difficulty remains, that it is extremely hard to believe in these things if they haven't been experienced; and of course, so it should be. It is very healthy to have a skeptical mind and to not believe everything we come across. Sometimes drastic things happen; people see shadows, faces, or even people they later realize weren't human, or they hear or feel things, but these are mostly rare. Much of this happens beyond the five senses and is extremely subtle.

What 'Attacks'?

A psychic attack is not always a possession, where a soul takes over a person and causes a complete change in behavior. Not every energy out there is a 'soul', but there are many fragments of energy that have a life of their own because of the energy we/ others have given it. For example if someone lived in a house harboring intense hatred for many years, someone moving in after them will experience unreasonable hatred, and even more so when they are vulnerable.

One could be affected by simply negative energy, an entity or a spirit. An entity is a fragment of energy that was created as a result of a strong dissatisfaction due to unfulfilled desires or disappointments. A spirit is the energy of a dead person which has been unable to move on due to strong attachment to a person, emotion or idea. It is not strong enough to possess someone but capable enough to use another person to satisfy their desires.

When affected by negative energy, a person might feel dull, negative or get sick for a few days. Most people are capable of dealing with negative energy given a few days. Entities and spirits affect people for much longer and if they are intelligent forces, they can even go undetected for years. I have met people who show no signs of being affected even to psychics, because the energy is well-masked.

Myths about Psychic Attacks

Psychic attack is a scary subject, even for many healers. As a result, we develop many belief systems to help us feel safe and pretend like nothing bad can happen.

If you don't believe in them, they can't hurt you

If you didn't believe in viruses, would that mean you would never catch a cold? No, but it might mean that you wouldn't go to a doctor for treatment. Of course, one can only believe what one has experienced, but a strong belief that 'such things' don't exist, and that believing in their non-existence will somehow protect you, is quite the opposite of what really happens. Such a belief will prevent a person from acknowledging a real problem and seeking help when required.

If you believe nothing can hurt you, nothing can

While normal people prefer to believe that all of this is fantasy, many healers prefer to believe that if one believes one is strong enough, nothing can affect them. It ultimately has the same consequence as the previous belief – it prevents a person from acknowledging what is going on and seeking help at the right time.

If you believe in God, nothing can harm you

If you have a very strong spiritual practice, it does minimize your chances of picking up something vicious. But more often than not, I find people who say a 5 minute prayer a day or light a candle or lamp living under the illusion that their belief in God is enough to protect them. Belief is not enough, a strong practice is a must to be able to benefit from grace.

The fact is, things can go wrong. Not just in the spirit world, but also in the material world. Rich people can suddenly lose all of their money and have to sleep on the sidewalk – their money is not an insurance against not so good times. Someone you have loved all your life could turn against you or cheat you out of the blue – your love isn't an insurance for their affection. Just when you think your life is finally settled, everything could be destroyed in a war or a flood. Things go wrong. And things can go wrong spiritually too. No amount of spiritual practice or belief system is an insurance against psychic or life problems, and the sooner we deal with this fact, the better we will be at coping with life.

Entities/ spirits have evil intentions

We watch horror movies and assume that all disembodied spirits out there want to entertain themselves at our expense. That is far from the truth. In many cases, spirits are disturbed, lost and merely seeking help. Some are even tremendously grateful and say thank you before they leave towards the light. In some cases they might be malicious, but that is fairly rare and it definitely doesn't play out the way horror movies portray it to be.

This happens only to people

It is not always easy to detect a psychic attack, even in a person. Animals are also prone to psychic attacks and I have had clients whose pets displayed abnormal strength when under the influence, later calming down to their normal docile selves once remedial measures were taken. If pets start acting unusually aggressive, it is a good idea to do a thorough cleansing of the house.

This happens only to *weak* people

Just like not everyone sick is a 'weak' person, not everyone experiencing a psychic attack is weak. In fact, most people who get affected are not only physically strong, but also have very strong minds and have displayed extreme discipline at other points in their lives. Those who are weak through prolonged or intense illness, or due to a mental disorders are certainly very easy targets. However, a moment of weakness can be all that is needed if one happens to be in the wrong place at the wrong time.

Also, when people start growing, they come face to face with their own shadow, which can destabilize them for a short while and if they are unlucky, they get affected. People can seem very weak and dysfunctional when they are affected, but it is quite a different story when they are completely healed.

Mental Disorders are a Result of Psychic Attack

There are many similarities in the symptoms of mental disorders and psychic attacks. Not all people under psychic attack will be diagnosed with mental disorders, and not all people with mental disorders are under psychic attack. There are a few differences, and sometimes people with serious mental disorders can be under attack, making their condition a lot worse. Just like not believing in psychic attack prevents a person from seeking the right help in time, not believing in medical science can prevent a person from getting the right help in time. When things get difficult, it is important to check with a mental health practitioner.

What Makes Us Vulnerable?

Psychic attacks do not happen just like that. In fact, there is nothing more unfortunate than a person who is not under psychic attack passing off the responsibility of fixing a problem by thinking that it is all happening because of things out of his control.

Some people are naturally more susceptible to psychic attacks, and some are susceptible only during certain moments in life. I have known many people who are very well grounded and none of the things listed below affect them. The weaker a person is, the most these things will affect them. As a healer I have met people who have been affected by every single factor listed below.

Emotional Instability

One of the biggest causes for psychic attacks is an emotionally weak state. When a person is emotionally broken down or under a great deal of stress, their auric defenses are extremely weak and can be violated very easily. Someone who has just lost a loved one to death or has just been abandoned by a loved one is particularly vulnerable. Such a person will have some strong unfulfilled desire and if this resonates with a similar entity, the attraction is very strong and one gets affected. Loneliness is another emotion that leaves people open, because they're willing to let anyone in to feel like they're not alone.

Environment

There are two factors in psychic attacks. One, how weak or strong are you? And two, is there a spirit or entity nearby that might be interested in you? Where you are, greatly influences the second factor. If you live in a space which is thoroughly cleansed and has a strong energy field, you are already quite safe. However, when you are in a place full of entities or spirits, a slight slip can leave you affected. I once met a person who went to a cemetery with friends in a moment of bravado after a few drinks. It was a disaster and he came back almost incoherent. His other friends were unaffected. Passing through forests in the dark can also be risky, as can be watching horror shows – for some people.

Some places are more prone to have entities present than others:

- Forests and trees at night
- Lone trees in vast open spaces
- Houses or rooms that have been empty for a long time
- Houses or rooms of people who have been depressed/ ill for a long time. Sleeping in the bed of such a person could be quite detrimental for a sensitive person.
- Places where people have been tortured or killed before
- Cemeteries

Sex

Sex is not just a physical process, it exposes both people to each other's energies and entities easily move from one person to another during intercourse. The energy connection does not end with the end of physical contact, or even with the end of a relationship. An energetic connection is retained with one's sexual partners, the strength of this connection depending on the intensity of the relationship while it lasted.

Menstrual Cycles

Women are highly prone to psychic attack during their

monthly period, which is why many cultures isolate women during this time. Going to places of worship is a definite no-no for various reasons. The one relevant to our topic is that people come to sacred places to let go of their baggage. While in general this works fine because sacred places hold a high energy, a woman's energy field is sensitive enough during this time to pick up what other people are releasing before it gets balanced out by the energy field of the place. It is best to avoid places where you generally feel weak or tired during this time.

Psychic Activity

Engaging in psychic activity like telepathically communicating with someone creates channels of energy connecting people, and these forces can easily travel from one continent to another through such openings. Deliberately indulging in psychic activity such as using Ouija boards, mediumship, out of body experiences or lucid dreaming can leave a person exposed and sometimes leave them affected for years.

Healing

Feeling very sympathetic again opens up a person to another's energy, as do some systems of healing. If the technique of healing you use involves a lot of cleansing rituals, rest assured that that is because such a system leaves you very exposed. Some healing systems are more effective in sending dark energies directly to the light, whereas others require more involvement from the healer, which can be risky if he healer is not well-grounded.

Intoxicants

Merely drinking alcohol might not affect a person much, but being in an inebriated state opens one up to these influences. Drugs damage the system the most, eroding the protective lining of the aura and leaving a person completely open to attack.

Antiques

Antique items carry with them the energy of the previous owner and must be thoroughly cleansed before they are used. Items like mirrors and beds carry the most powerful remnants. Filling up one's home with antique items exposes one to these energies and there can be problems if the items aren't cleansed and if anyone in the house is sensitive or temporarily has a weak aura.

Other Factors

Most people find this hard to believe, even more so because it interferes with our lifestyles, but leaving hair untied especially after dusk leaves one very exposed and vulnerable, as hair act like antenna picking up information and energy from our surroundings. Wearing perfume also weakens one's aura drastically. These are things I have observed even psychics to be unaware of, but if you have any psychic ability, carefully observe the energy of a person before and after a party. If the person wore perfume and their hair loose, the difference in energy is very clear. Sleeping with such energy without a shower will let the energy settle in and affect the person in the long term. These factors don't affect men with the intensity with which it affects women. If you are a sensitive woman, avoid synthetic perfumes and keep your hair tied up as much as possible.

Weaknesses in the Horoscope

Very frequently, there is a connection between the astrological outline of a person's life and how prone they are to psychic attacks. This is not to say that a person's horoscope indicates a story set in stone, but it can give insights into times where a person is very vulnerable and this information can be useful to have.

People with certain weaknesses in their charts remain prone to psychic attacks almost all of their lives. Others find themselves vulnerable only for a certain period of time, ranging from a few weeks to a few years. If this kind of information is known in advance, one can be extra careful by not indulging in risky activity as outlined above.

Sometimes there are astrological solutions, but it is better to be careful before one explores expensive astrological remedies and ensure that the astrologer is truly trustworthy.

Symptoms of Psychic Attack

Entities can attach themselves to people and remain there quietly for years without anyone finding out. If they are highly disturbed energies, or if the energy of the person carrying the entity is so high that it is making the entity uncomfortable, it might make its presence felt.

Here are few signs you might be under external influence. Take care to note that some of the factors mentioned below might be a part of a person's nature. However, if they are usually uncharacteristic, then it indicates that something is wrong. For example, some people are naturally messy, but when a person who is normally particular about neatness suddenly finds it extremely burdensome to clear up the house, it is quite likely a sign.

You are Thinking Unusual Thoughts

One effect of a strong psychic attack is the presence of horrible thoughts, which don't feel one's own. One often wonders 'what is wrong with me? I never think like this'. If you are suddenly experiencing irrational thoughts that don't feel like they are yours, they are probably not.

Difficulty in Maintaining a Spiritual Practice

For those who have a fairly regular spiritual practice, this is the easiest indication. When affected by external energies, there is a sudden drop in desire for any spiritual practice and one would make silly excuses to skip it. One has to almost force oneself into the practice and even then it feels like a half-hearted attempt. There is a loss of interest in any activity that helps raise one's energies.

Loss of Memory

The memory gets affected in strange ways. Either parts of

one's past get erased or incidents that would normally be remembered are wiped off from the memory. At other times, one becomes very absent-minded, forgetting where one left the keys, misplacing things, etc.

Disorientation/ Brain-Fog/ Headaches

Being under the influence of external energies can mess with your head if you are not grounded enough. People can find it difficult to think, almost as if it takes too much energy and feeling as if the head is fogged up and heavy, sometimes even having a headache when trying too hard. Some can feel a dull pressure or throbbing inside the head, as if something is pushing against the walls of the skull from inside.

Excessive Fatigue

Entities that take over feed on our energy and leave little room for activity. A persistent weakness and a lack of desire to participate in life is a very common symptom. In combination with the disorientation, it can make a person quite incapable of functioning normally.

Unusual or Excessive Sleep

The excessive fatigue often leads to very deep, heavy sleep and one wakes up with the whole body feeling heavy and no matter how long one sleeps, it never feels enough and one wakes up feeling drained.

This is not the only way sleep gets affected, though. Some people respond to psychic attack by finding themselves unable to sleep due to a subconscious fear of a presence in the room. They might only fall asleep in the wee hours of the morning or have fragmented sleep. Nightmares are also common, and dreams are very vivid.

Choking/ Pressure/ Burning

A repetitive feeling of choking, muscle spasms or pressure, usually on the chest is also a common symptom. There may also be burning sensations in some parts of the body.

Physical Problems with no Medical Diagnosis

In extreme cases or if the person is weak, an entity attachment can result in physical problems, and in many cases there is nothing wrong physically when medical tests are done. However, it could also manifest as thyroid or uterus issues in women. Other common physical symptoms are feeling of sharp pains, throbbing, tightness, a sinking feelings or waking up with unexplained bruises often in the shape of a bite. Psychic attacks also reflect in the eyes; the eyes seem darker, heavier, and dark circles might suddenly appear.

Strong Desire for Sensual Gratification/ Fetishes/ Addictions

Entities inhabit bodies primarily for some sort of physical gratification. Many people tend to naturally depend on physical gratification, and this is not a sign of psychic attack. It is a clear sign though, if this desire for gratification is sudden and unusual. For example when a person who normally enjoys eating healthy starts craving for junk food. Or when some starts having an unusually high desire for sex. One might develop sudden, strange fetishes or OCD-like behaviors for no apparent reason. There might also be a tendency to get addicted to people who one knows aren't the right kind, or the sort one might not even be normally interested in, but one can't pull themselves away.

Unreasonable, Erratic Behavior

This happens more often to women. When someone starts to act completely out of character, turning into a (verbally or physically) violent person suddenly from a normally kind and loving person, it signals psychic trouble. Sometimes this violent behavior could be directed at oneself too. In most cases I have observed that this kind of behavior in a woman is accompanied by uterus problems.

Hearing Sounds/ Seeing Shadows/ Feeling Touched or Watched

Depending on the predominant sense of the person, he or she might hear, see or sense a presence. One might hear voices, thuds, footsteps or creaks. One might see orbs, lights, shadows or in extreme cases hallucinate. One might feel touched or patted at times, or feel sensations like feather-touch all over the limbs while in bed. Sometimes there are very foul smells that clearly don't have a source.

There might be a feeling of being watched, or cold sensations all over the body. Some people see an eye or a pair of eyes looking at them when they close their eyes, and others can start to get paranoid that they're being watched wherever they are.

Receiving Information You Never Had

In slightly extreme cases, people can receive blasts of information and images that are not their own. Very infrequently this happens when people are channeling divine beings, but in such a cases it is very easy to stop the flow. But more often than not, these are just mischievous spirits masquerading as light beings and giving people an illusion that they are transmitting real information.

I've had clients who believed they could read people's minds because they could 'hear' their thoughts, clients who believed that they were enlightened because they had some bizarre experiences and others who believed that they were being given information about the future or receiving information from God. While the most susceptible people to this phenomenon are those who channel, I have also seen this happen with people who have a very weak self-esteem and a strong desire to be spiritually superior to everyone else. Spirits can play into the victim's desire to feel special, and often convey to them messages like 'you are sent to earth with a very special purpose'. Authentic divine beings know that we are all equal and will not allow for any feelings of superiority. Any genuine instructions will be action-based, and not label-based (for e.g. 'spend more time healing people', vs. 'you are a light-worker/ star-seed/ anything else')

Fluctuating with the Moons

Full moons and new moons increase the amount of energy the earth is receiving, and this makes external energies uncomfortable. The result is higher levels of restlessness, and subsequently stronger reactions. If you are experiencing any of the problems mentioned above and if they get stronger around full and new moons, it is a definite sign that you are under attack.

If any of these are happening to you, that is if they aren't part of your basic nature, it is a sign you need some strong cleansing and need to intensify your spiritual practice manifold until you find yourself stable and strong again. Those who are generally prone need to ensure they consistently maintain a strong spiritual practice.

Pets Acting Strangely

Animals can sense energies and if there is a sudden change in the way they respond to you, there may be reason for alarm. Animals or even little children might look at spots in the room with a fixed stare. This happens sometimes even normally, but if the child/ dog looks ready to attack or scared, then it might be something to be careful of. If the animal is under psychic attack it could be unduly aggressive, might get a mysterious physical illness or may act as if it doesn't know or recognize the pet-parent. Even well-trained dogs can completely forget their toilet and behavior training during this phase and the memory comes back after healing.

Types of Psychic Attack

Before we try to heal someone with psychic attack, it is helpful to know exactly what type of attack it is. The mild ones can be resolved quite easily and there is no need to as they say, kill a mosquito with a shotgun.

General Negativity

We tend to be careless sometimes, especially when with people we love or in intimidating environments. If the person we are talking to is depressed or anxious, we might pick up their energy. This will be further intensified if we feel sympathetic towards them. Similarly if we spend some time in a negative space we could feel low and lethargic by the time we leave. Walking barefoot on grass or taking a shower the moment you are back home should solve this problem.

I have had clients who were seeing too many things or feelings things that weren't coherent with what they were actually experiencing in the physical realm, and we found out that it wasn't psychic attack that was their problem, but a punctured, over sensitized aura which was picking up the emotions and thoughts of everyone around them, even neighbors. In such a case the person needs a very strong focus on strengthening the aura through grounding and slow yoga.

Energetic Cords

Intense or long-term emotional dependency can create energetic cords that drain our energy. We tend to look at being needed as an important aspect of life. Most people I have worked with, tell me that if no one needed them in the world, life would feel quite worthless. A desire to be needed is really a desire to be validated through another person. One cannot need and love at the same time, and in a need-based relationship people are loyal to needs, not to the person fulfilling them.

A need-based relationship thus essentially becomes a business deal, where one fulfills a certain need in exchange for affection. It starts to become quite a strain over a period of time, because both people start to take the other for granted. Energetically what is going on is that a cord has been established between two people, with both willingly giving energy to the other in the beginning. However, as time passes, both want to take more than they give, and the stronger one eventually wins, leaving the other feeling drained and tired.

Healers are Quite Prone, Too

Being a healer is not always an easy task as we come across many people experiencing deep suffering. Most teachers explain to their students that feeling sympathy for a client is a strict no-no, but reality is quite different. In even more unfortunate cases, healers block out sympathy and simply refuse to feel anything but positive emotions for a client. This causes suppression and over time will cause disease. Suppression or not, every healer feels sympathetic at some point or the other. Being aware of what is going on inside oneself can make one more equipped to do something about it.

Sympathy creates attachments in the form of energetic cords. Some healers cut cords at the end of every healing session, but this is not always the only source. A phone call from a distressed person, thoughts about a client who is still in pain after many sessions and other such situations would still create cords.

Over a period of time, there are too many cords and the healer might feel tired and almost allergic to seeing any more clients. Cord-cutting is a wonderful technique that can help in this situation in the short term. In the long term one needs to look deeply at what is bringing about that sympathy and gently heal what comes up.

The 'Evil Eye'

I have found this to be common in cultures where there is less respect for personal space. It is usually unintentional and it could even happen through a loved one. The basic premise of the 'evil eye' is a feeling of lack in one person, and a (conscious or subconscious) desire to invoke envy in the other. In a situation like this, the energy exchange that happens between the two people leads to some sort of disturbance. For example, a person shows someone their new watch and later in the day, the watch breaks. This is a mild example, and the evil eye could affect a lot more than material possessions, sometimes creating physical problems for months. Those who feel good about themselves when being envied are the most susceptible to this.

Sensitive people will sense their energy getting heavy after they are affected by this. The eyes get heavy and suddenly there is no energy, usually quite a contrast from their energetic self a few hours or minutes before. Children are very easily affected and sudden fever is a very common symptom. Cheerful, happy babies suddenly get very cranky when affected and feel much heavier on being carried.

Psychic Attack by a Person

People can also attack each other psychically, both consciously and subconsciously.

Subconscious psychic attacks happen through repetitive aggressive or controlling behavior. If the victim is incapable of handling extremely emotional situations, it breaks their defenses down and leads to energetic cords between the two, through which energy is continuous leaked. The aggressor might use intense emotions such as hatred, anger, guilt, physical abuse to oneself or the other, and emotional blackmail to control the victim. The victim is left incapacitated, unable to think and usually living in fear of the next 'episode'.

In most cases this continuous fear creates a spate of secondary problems including physical disease and mental instability. In most cases the aggressor is mentally unstable or a victim of some sort of psychic attack and it is important not to make a demon out of them. They need help and care to be able to heal too, although the victim might need considerable time away to maximize the speed of recovery.

Conscious psychic attacks happen when someone who has been dabbling in occult sciences wants to gain control over someone. They may or may not be aware that such actions carry very serious karmic consequences. When it comes to control, it always involves a 'giver' and a 'receiver', where the 'giver' has the capacity to project thoughts and feelings onto other people and the 'receiver' is sensitive by nature, maybe even an empath. What follows is uncharacteristic behavior, with the victim often being uncharacteristically subdued and submissive, and/or feeling addicted to the sort of person they would normally never be interested in. In the short term, this leads to clouded thinking, and in the long term this starts to destroy their capacity to take decisions.

Wandering Spirits or Entities

If a person's aura is weak, there is a much higher chance of picking up stray energies. The aura weakens when a person is experiencing intense negative emotions. Picking up such energies will result in a desire for some sort of gratification, like a compulsive desire to binge on food, shopping, sex or alcohol, television or in some cases go into self-destruct mode, exercising too hard or working too many hours.

Sleep Paralysis

Sometimes people wake up in the middle of the night feeling a great weight on their chest or sometimes even seeing someone sitting on them. They realize very quickly that they cannot scream; indeed, they cannot even move. Obviously, this is extremely terrifying.

Some sleep paralysis can happen when a person wakes up in their astral body instead of the physical body. In this case, one finds that one is floating above the body looking down, or maybe lying down and trying to get up, but completely unable to move or talk. While most people perceive this as an extremely scary experience, this is not psychic attack, it is merely a sign that the person is beginning to travel astrally during sleep.

However, if there is a heavy weight on the chest or any other part of the body or if a dark presence is seen or felt, it is psychic attack. Sometimes the person is also used sexually, and it might be anything from caressing to penetration; this could happen to men as well as women, usually happens when there are suppressed sexual desires.

Curse or Black Magic

Many people I have met have serious doubts about the existence of black magic. Unfortunately, it is very real. I've observed a higher prevalence in India and Australia, and haven't come across too many such cases in Europe or America. Black magicians use a variety of tools to bring about results that a client desires, from herbs to blood, bones and spirits. When it is malevolent, it can be used to manipulate thoughts and actions, and create illness, financial problems, rift in relationships and even death. Some examples of people affected by black magic include husbands leaving wives for no apparent reason, babies dying mysteriously, successful businessmen suddenly unable to function, leaving everything to business partners and sitting at home doing nothing till the end of their lives, etc.

Possession

This is the most extreme manifestation of psychic attack and can be very hard to handle. Possession could happen on the long term or short term and can bring about many changes. In extreme cases there might be obvious changes in accent, voice and eye color, they may even look different. During short term possessions, people might even display super-human abilities. One of my clients had watched as her six year old son ran in circles around the courtyard in a frenzy, and when she tried to grab hold of him he hit her with one hand, hauling her right across the threshold. It was a short episode, and he was fine after she managed to press a sacred amulet onto his chest. Sometimes spirits move in and out, in which case the person will have no memory of the time when he or she was possessed. Animals tend to be afraid of such a person.

Preventing Psychic Attacks

If we ensure our aura is strong and stable, we minimize our vulnerability to psychic attacks. Even when try to heal psychic attack, it helps to start with the steps mentioned below.

Awareness

Awareness is a very important aspect on the spiritual pathway. The most important advantage of being aware is that we find out very quickly when something goes wrong and we can take steps to correct it before things get too serious. The other advantage is that it brings us face to face with our shadow and enables us to acknowledge and integrate it. When a person is affected by negativity, awareness helps reduce the impact by helping us see through the thoughts instead of getting swept away by them.

Body-Work

Psychic attacks might manifest on the physical, mental or energy plane, but they always affect us on all levels. Working with the body ensures that the body remains clean and there are no 'pockets' for the energy to settle in. Understand that all the extremely rigid parts of your body are vulnerable to attack. Also, pain is an indication that energy is not flowing smoothly in that part. Bringing awareness into these parts of our body continuously opens the energy up and creates space for healing. Slow yoga is great for strengthening the energy system and so is dancing. For those who live in warm, humid climates, activities like going to the gym and running can weaken the system.

Staying Grounded

This is absolutely *the* most powerful thing that can keep psychic attacks at bay. Spending time in nature, hugging trees with your spine touching the trunk of the tree. Another exercise that helps is to imagine a red glowing sun in the tip of the tailbone, growing larger on the in-breath and shrinking a bit on the out-breath, as if this red sun is pulsating with the breath. If the mind wanders, we gently bring it back to this. At the end we can imagine that this red energy is flowing through our legs into our feet and into the center of the earth, forming roots like a tree. This needs to be done every day.

A Strong Spiritual Practice

Spirituality is not about positivity. Positive energy is not a source of protection, balanced and stable energies are. It is important to understand the difference. A strong spiritual practice would involve some sort of 'practice', like maybe a self-healing or meditation, but that is not all. It needs to be a way of living. There is no spirituality without surrender. Increasingly, chasing goals are being projected as a part of the spiritual pathway, under the guise of 'everyone deserves to live well'. But more often than not, this is shrouded in lack of surrender and a focus on the void in one's life in the absence of fulfilled desires. It is important not to fight anything – life-situations, emotions, or physical disease.

Shadow-Work

Each and every one of us has a 'shadow', a collection of our deepest, darkest thoughts and feelings that we're so afraid to acknowledge that we pretend they don't exist. The bigger a person's shadow, the more prone they are to a psychic attack. This is why people who are new on the spiritual pathway are the most vulnerable, because they confuse being spiritual with being good, and pretend like they have no darkness. This becomes a gaping weakness and can very easily be used to drain energy from a person.

Watch Out for Dependencies

Whether we are running away (from the shadow) or running towards something very intensely, it creates scope for manipulation. Watch very closely if you are highly dependent on anything – spouse, kids, close friends, objects, shopping, or the TV or internet. If someone else is highly dependent on you, that counts too as we create dependencies because there's a strong subconscious desire to be needed. If you identify any such dependencies, work actively on learning to stand up on your own feet either by yourself or with help from a therapist.

Bubbles, Shields and Flooding

When we know that we will be spending time with people or in situations that tend to drain our energy, we could protect ourselves using imaginary bubbles or shields. However, I have found that these work only some of the times, and I personally prefer flooding much more as it comes more from love than from fear and separation.

Healing Psychic Attack

Healing by Type

General Negativity

Simple negativity is fairly easy to remove. Leaning on a tree with our back resting on the trunk, walking on the grass, taking a shower when we get home, or even simply flooding oneself with light is enough to wash away anything we have picked up.

Energetic Cords

Dealing with cords on the long term requires some deep introspection to investigate what emotional need was being fulfilled. When a person gives too much of herself, she feels that she was actually gaining nothing from the relationship and there was only a one way flow of energy. This is far from the truth, and such people actually have a strong desire to be needed – and this need has to be acknowledged, accepted and healed. Until this happens, cords will keep forming either with the same or a different person. For a short term solution, cord-cutting is useful, and is discussed in the next chapter.

The 'Evil Eye'

Adults tend to feel tired and often display a very strong desire to take a nap immediately after getting home. This must be avoided as it makes it much harder to cleanse the energies. Taking a shower and using rock salt to cleanse one's energies might be enough. If there is still a heavy feeling, it would help to hug a tree with the spine aligned with the trunk of the tree, although this shouldn't be done after dusk. If it is late in the evening, smudging the aura with sage will help.

Psychic Attack by a Person

When being attacked by a person, the best solution is to avoid meeting that person completely. If meeting is inevitable, avoid eye contact and long conversations. The awareness that one is being attacked itself starts to weaken the influence. Bring your focus to the movement of your belly as you breathe. This will help you ground yourself in your body and prevent mental manipulation. Whenever you feel like doing or saying something, ask if this is really what you want to do or say.

Wandering Spirits or Entities

Cleanse your aura and space every evening just after dusk. Cleansing techniques will be discussed in the next chapter, and using fire is the best option. Along with this, chanting sacred mantras regularly will help strengthen your aura. Any meditation should be exclusively on the lower chakras, avoid focusing on the upper chakras. Regular Reiki healing goes a long way in healing entity problems.

Sometimes healers are capable of healing more than just human beings, and spirits can sense this. If this is the case, spirits might reach out to a healer for help. It isn't psychic attack in such a case, but there might be nightmares if a healer hasn't become aware of the spirit's presence. They're just reaching out for help and sending them some healing along with instructions that it is safe for them to go back to the light is usually enough.

Sleep Paralysis

If you ever find yourself awake and unable to move your body, breathe irregularly. Breath is the only thing that connects the different bodies and is also the only thing that can be manipulated. Take irregular long and short breaths, and you will soon find yourself back in control. If there is a demonic presence around, chanting a mantra or calling out to your favorite deities/ angels is very helpful.

Curse or Black Magic

Black magic can be of various intensities. If it is not too intense, simply learning Reiki and practicing everyday can lead to huge improvements and reduce the impact of the black magic to almost nil. However, if it is very strong, either the help of a good wizard/ *tantric* is required, or one needs to religiously perform sacred rituals every day to keep harm at bay.

Possession

To be able to help with black magic or possession, the healer needs to be extremely experienced. It is not something I recommend healers to try unless they are very confident that they can handle it. If you are experiencing possession, then work on strengthening your aura through very slow yoga, chanting, connecting with nature and strong meditation on the root.

General Steps for Healing Psychic Attacks

Love

Fear is the biggest hindrance in working with any type of psychic attack. These problems evoke fear, and entities even often use fear to get us back into control. The problem is, they feed on fear. They heal and eventually go back to the source, with love. It is important to understand that whether it is a person or a spirit or an entity attacking us, they are doing so because they are controlled by their own fears. Whenever they appear in your thoughts or whenever you feel their presence, wish them love and peace, and shower them with white, pink or golden light. You might want to say *"go back to the light, it is safe and peaceful"* if you feel connected to the energy in any way.

If you have learned level 2 Reiki, you could send them healing every day, otherwise you could do flooding when you feel the presence. We will learn flooding in the next chapter.

Breathing Deeply

One of the unfortunate aspects of our ideas of beauty is the habit of tucking in our bellies. This causes us to breathe only through the upper part of our lungs, making our breath very shallow. Your breath is a clear indicator of the life force energy (*prana*) in your body. The lesser the *prana*, the weaker you are physically, mentally, emotionally, and energetically.

Make it a habit to breathe from the depths of your belly. Practice full yogic breathing, where you sit in a comfortable position with your spine erect, breathe out to empty your lungs, and then breathe in by first expanding your belly, then your lungs, and then raising your shoulders. Hold your breath for 1 to 5 seconds and breathe out in the reverse order, collapsing your shoulders, contracting your lungs and then your belly. Repeat a few times. Practice it so it becomes almost natural, of course without the exaggerated movements.

Watch Your Thoughts Very Carefully

Entities and spirits affect your mind first. It is of prime importance to learn not to pursue the thoughts appearing in the mind. Your weaknesses will be exaggerated and whatever it is you are prone to feeling, whether guilt, depression, anger or something else, will be brought up with much more intensity. As one of my clients put it, it messes with your inner radar and you don't know what to trust anymore, because your internal guidance can no longer be trusted. It is a difficult place to be in, but question every thought in your mind and ask if you really need to be thinking this. Avoid any thoughts related to past or future and only allow thinking to happen when you need work to be done.

Another line of thought to be careful of is thoughts about the entity itself. I have seen many people get curious and want to find out about the spirit/ entity. What or who is it, where did it come from, why is it affecting me? The mind loves stories and seeks answers so that it can create more questions. Not only is the pursuit of such thoughts pointless as they don't lead you towards the solution, but they actually connect you more deeply with the attachment.

Remember this: when you think about anyone, whether positive or negative thoughts, you establish an open channel of energy with that person or entity. This channel can be used by the person if they have strong psychic abilities, and definitely will be used by the entity to take up more of your energy. Do not suppress fearful, worrisome or curious thoughts about entities, but redirect your mind towards your body through one of the grounding exercises mentioned towards the end of the book.

Visiting a Sacred Space

Sometimes this can be very helpful if the place is very powerful. If you feel deeply connected with a place of worship, visiting it frequently can greatly help in clearing your aura. It is important to ensure you remain grounded while over there and especially while leaving so as to not reverse the benefit.

Go Vegetarian

I am not particularly pro-vegetarianism or veganism, but I have observed it to make a significant difference among people under psychic attack. All kinds of meat lower the vibrations of the body and help create space for the entities to exist. Red meats, especially beef and pork are particularly quick in weakening the aura. Until you are completely cleansed and have regained your strength, it is advisable to keep foods simple and vegetarian.

Holy Water, Holy Ash

Sprinkling holy water can be quite quick sometimes in calming down someone under psychic attack. Applying holy ash or ash from sacred fire rituals over the third eye is very effective in preventing psychic attack, as that is the entry-point for entities. Other substitutes are vermillion or sandalwood paste.

Angels

It can be helpful to call upon Angels when feeling threatened. In many Eastern countries, people have family deities, and these are the most powerful forces that can help swiftly and effectively. If you're not aware of your family deity, simply call out to your favorite God, angel or deity.

If you feel more connected with Christian culture, you might choose to call upon Archangel Michael for protection, Archangel Raphael for healing and Archangel Uriel for wisdom and practical solutions. If it is Hindu culture that draws you, you would want to pray to Goddess Gayatri to bring in the light and dispel darkness, Goddess Kali or Durga to destroy the demons, and Hanuman for protection and developing auric strength. Buddhist Dakini Simhamukha is invoked specifically to avert psychic attack. Ekajati and Avalokiteshvara also help with protection. Among Egyptian deities, Isis, Horus, Serket can help. This is only a small list, there are many more.

You might even choose to call upon a combination of these forces and it has nothing to do with religion, which is only man-made boundaries. However, we always find it easier to connect with certain forces and it is more effective to connect with those which you feel drawn to, than to those which books tell you are good for you.

You may choose to seek the grace of these forces in many different ways:

- Place a photograph or some other object representing them
- Imagine them in front of you and request healing/ guidance/ protection
- Chant related mantras or prayers, or simply chant their name repeatedly
- If you have repetitive problems, it helps to chant related mantras or prayers daily.

Crystals

Crystals are a very important aspect of healing psychic attacks, especially for healers. I have come across many people and healers who have a tendency to indulge in crystal retail-therapy, but lack the patience to clear the crystals on a regular basis. This is extremely dangerous, as crystals act as amplifiers. Once they pick up toxic energies, they amplify the effect of that too, and they also act as 'houses' for stray spirits that match that vibration. I have met people who were having recurrent nightmares and got better immediately after they removed all the crystals from their bedside after I asked them to.

If the psychic attack is very severe or it seems to be affecting the household through relationship or financial problems, try removing all the crystals from the house, putting them in a cloth bag and leaving them inside a hole in the earth in your garden. This cannot be a balcony, it has to be outside the walls of your house. Make sure you cleanse your house thoroughly after this, with rock salt or a fire cleanse.

Leave the crystals out there for three days and if things get better, you know what the source of the problem was. Many even experience a sudden relief even in the material sense, the very next day! A few weeks later if you wish, you can take out the crystals, leave them to charge in the full moon and use them if you still want to, just make sure you cleanse them twice a month or so, or every week if you are a healer.

Crystals can help with protection if used right. In situations like psychic attack, they need to be cleansed and charged every day, and are mainly useful if the victim does not know how to heal himself or herself. Cleanse the crystal by leaving it overnight in a bowl of rock salt, and charge it by giving Reiki or passing it over the fumes or smoke when performing fire rituals. Hang the crystal around your neck or wrist during the day and it will help keep you safe. Black Tourmaline, Smoky Quartz, Black Kyanite and Black Obsidian help with protection. Rose Quartz helps to convert negative emotions to positive. I do not recommend Amethyst for this purpose.

The Most Important Aspect for Healing and Protection

The importance of a daily spiritual practice cannot be understated. As mentioned earlier, one of the first things a person experiences is a complete loss of interest in the daily spiritual practice. Those who are connected with an uplifting teacher or a group will suddenly lose touch and be unable to join them. There is in fact, a strong resistance to do absolutely anything that might help heal from the psychic attack, and there might even be obstacles every time a person tries something.

These obstacles can range from simple boredom or painful spasms during spiritual practice, to cars breaking down when trying to shop for items necessary for a cleansing ritual. In many instances if one has had a strong spiritual practice, the momentum that has created protects one for a while and one can take this for granted.

However, one eventually runs out of grace if nothing is being done to stabilize the aura and things can suddenly get worse when this happens. One needs a strong resolve to keep up the spiritual practice no matter what.

If you practice Reiki, it is important to ensure you heal the front as well as back chakras, and that the lower chakras get more healing time than upper chakras. Many healers tend to take short-cuts and find quicker methods of healing, but short-cuts never bring you the complete results. In my experience so far, I have found without exception that every short-cut method of healing only offers a fraction of the benefit that a minimum 30-minute full body Reiki healing offers. I have observed that those who spend half an hour healing in the evening and an additional 20-30 minutes in the morning develop the most stable auras.

Healing is not Always Pleasant

If one is under the influence of a fairly intense psychic attack, there can be a backlash the moment a remedy is tried. If the psychic attack wasn't too strong, remedial measures work immediately and the problem is resolved, and one only needs to be careful for the next few days to ensure that there is no subsequent attack while the body heals.

When the healing is not strong enough to remove the influence, the entity of spirit fights back through the only tool it has – fear. People can experience extreme fatigue, sudden worsening of mental or physical symptoms, untimely onset of menstrual cycles, nightmares and visions or sounds.

The only way is to keep at it, and not give in to the fear. Intensify the daily spiritual practice and make sure fire cleansing is done every day until the problem disappears.

Some Useful Techniques

Rock Salt Cleanse

This is probably one of the easiest, quickest cleansing methods. If you are healing someone else who seems to have plenty of negative energy, place a bowl of rock salt under the bed or massage table. If you have picked up negative energy, here's a simple process:

- Take a couple of spoons of rock salt in your palm and close it into a fist.
- Place this fist on the top of your head and request the universe to cleanse any negativity affecting your thoughts.
- Place the fist on your heart and request the universe to cleanse and neutralize any impact on your emotions and relationships.
- Now place it on your root chakra and request the universe to heal and re-establish your connection with the earth.
- Flush this salt immediately. Do not throw it in a bin.

If you have learned Reiki level 2, you may draw all the symbols at every step of this process.

Epsom Salt

Epsom salt is great for cleansing the aura. To make the most of it, add four generous handfuls to a tub full of warm water, along with essential oils like sage, sandalwood or cedar. Of course, dim lights, candles and soothing music will deepen relaxation and enable you to release more. Soak in it for at least fifteen to twenty minutes, take a shower and moisturize your body immediately as the salts can dry the skin up a bit.

If a long-drawn bath is not an option, you could fill a large bowl with water, add a couple of tablespoons of Epsom salts and let it sit while you shower. Just before the end, pour it all over your body except the head, and rinse quickly in the shower. Soaking your feet in a tub of water with a couple tablespoons of Epsom salts is another option.

Quick Reiki Shower Cleanse

While we usually take a shower or a bath to cleanse the body physically, it is a great time to also cleanse our energies.

Apart from just charging the water, it helps to also regularly Reiki charge the soap or body wash you are using (or bath salts/ oil in case you are running a bath).

- Place your hands near the shower head and mentally draw all the symbols on it, requesting Reiki to charge all the water that flows through it for the next few minutes.
- Allow Reiki to flow through your palms as you lather/ rinse.
- Once you are done showering, stand so that the water falls on the top of your head.
- Imagine that the water is flowing into your body through the top of your head and cleansing away any energy blocks. If there is a block, most people find it hard to imagine the water flowing freely through that area.
- Become aware of your aura, and imagine that the water is also cleansing your energies all around your body.

• Draw the power symbol on all four or all six sides to seal the freshness.

Letting Nature Help

Nature is very helpful in restoring disturbed energies. However, we must take care not to walk in a forest or amidst trees after dusk as the energies shift considerably. Here are a few ways of taking the help of nature to heal.

• Walk barefoot on the grass, being completely aware of every sensation in the feet.

• Hug a tree backwards, aligning the spine with the trunk and requesting the tree to reconnect you deeply with the earth. This must not be done too many times with the same tree if one is undergoing chemotherapy, for it may kill the tree.

• Lying on the beach and swimming in the ocean are very helpful too, especially if done with the intent of reconnecting with the earth. When you enter the water, request mother earth to reconnect with you.

• If possible, the best way to heal is to spend a few continuous weeks in nature. It restores almost everything to balance.

• If there is negligible access to nature and parks, the concrete jungle can help too. Listen to the hum or traffic and tell yourself that this sound will have the same effect on you as the sound of the ocean. Look at pillars and tell yourself that your body will react in the same way to pillars as it does to trees. Repetition strengthens this and eventually your body stops getting stressed at the sounds of modernization.

Cutting Cords

Cord cutting can be done with a single person or with multiple people if we don't know whom we have cords with. Some healers believe that one mustn't cut cords with family members, but this is not correct. Energetic connections create dependencies and ultimately help no one. Without cords, close relationships are healthier, more open and more loving.

Let us first look at how to cut cords with a single person.

- Create a sacred space. You could light a few lamps or candles - lamps with cow's ghee (clarified butter) or sesame oil are said to be the most *satvik* (positive). Flowers would be good, incense if you like it.
- Start by observing your breath and entering a meditative space.
- Now imagine yourself in a circle, with the person sitting in front of you, also inside the circle. Slowly allow yourself become aware of the cords attaching the two of you.
- Pick one cord at a time, and ask yourself why you allowed this attachment to form. What was the fear that caused it, and what was the benefit you gained.
- It may be a good idea to ask the other person if they have anything to add. If you can seek permission before cutting every cord and if they are resisting, find out why and resolve that issue, then the cord cutting will bring you much more benefit.
- Once the reason for the presence of the cord is resolved, it may disappear by itself. If not, allow your intuition to guide you to the best way of cutting this cord. Once the cord is cut, burn the remains.
- Thank the person for teaching you valuable lessons, and ask them to leave the circle.
- Complete the process by doing a full self-healing. Cord cutting can sometimes leave a little soreness in the aura, and self-healing will heal any such wounds.

For healers who are used to working with energy, the process is slightly different.

- Create a sacred space and start with meditation.

- Once you feel stable and clear, look at yourself in your mind's eye and request to be shown all cords connected with you.

- Once you see the cords, follow your intuition on how they need to be removed. Sometimes you might want to use different methods until all the cords are gone.

- Look carefully at yourself again and see if you observe any gaps in your energy field. You can fill these gaps intuitively with colors, positive emotions or imaginary healing balms, whatever feels right.

- End with a full-body self-healing.

If you're a healer but are not very psychic, make quick, sweeping motions in front of your body as if you're chopping off with your arms the chains attached to your body. Do this with the intention that any existing cords be cut off permanently and follow this up with a self-healing.

A few things to bear in mind

Cord-cutting is best done at dusk time, and may need to be repeated for a few days until no cords are seen in the beginning of the process. Cord-cutting isn't the end of the story, and new cords will be formed over time with the same or a new person if the root cause isn't resolved.

It is important to look at the fears and conditioning that caused the creation of the cords in the first place. One easy way to do this is to request Reiki every night just before going to sleep, to bring up all the emotional issues that led to the creation of cords. Once the emotions are identified, meditate upon them and accept them as they are, without resistance and without trying to make them go away.

Sometimes the revelation that it was our own fears strengthening these bonds can be quite disturbing. If this is the case, I suggest that you let go of the idea of cutting cords for a few days, and allow Reiki to heal the resistance to these emotions, first.

If there are too many cords, you can cut a few every day and repeat this process for a few days until all cords are cut, and until no cords appear during the exercise. Sometimes one finds cords reappearing – this means it is a deep issue and needs more healing.

It is possible to cut cords without finding out the reasons and resolving them as well. However, the external world is nothing but a reflection of our inner selves, and blindly cutting cords might cause the same pattern to repeat again with another person. Ultimately, you chose to form those cords at a subconscious level. If you remove the reason, the problem heals more deeply.

Energy Flooding

This is a really effective and quick method for flooding people and situations with energy when we feel the need for a sudden energy boost. We might want to use it if we feel that a situation might go out of hand, or if we're interacting with someone who is either angry or upset with us, or just sucking out our energy.

The Method

Imagine energy pouring in through the top of your head, filling up your whole body with energy. Once your body is full, imagine that it starts to radiate the excess energy outwards, towards the person(s) in front of you, the whole room, or the situation.

The Idea

Life throws us many situations that might find us on the back foot. No matter what the situation, problems either begin or worsen if we give in to the reactions coming up within us. Flooding not only clears out our energy system, it also clears out the energy of the people in question, thereby creating a space for a calm and peaceful resolution.

Where we can use it

Here are some examples where flooding can be very useful

- To cleanse yourself and the people or space around you when you feel negative and low.
- When you feel an invisible negative presence nearby.
- If you feel ill or stuck with emotions that refuse to go away.
- If you find yourself trying to reason with a person who is swept away by emotion (e.g. angry, hysterical or being unreasonable)
- When you have to meet someone who dislikes you or makes you uncomfortable.
- When you have to address a group of people – in classrooms, in theatres, or in meetings and conference halls.
- For gatherings, parties and celebrations to go smoothly, flood the entire room with pink and green energies before the event, and then continue flooding the room at periodic intervals until it is over.
- While watching the news – when we feel agitated about the actions of people we haven't met, that is a very good time to practice some flooding. Not only will it clear out any negativity you might have picked

up but who knows, it might bring about some healing and some change in the person the news is about.

Bear in Mind

Using this technique is not about controlling someone. If that is the primary intention behind the flooding, then it might not be effective. Remember that we are first cleansing ourselves, so let that wash away any apprehensions we might have first, and then flood the other person to turn the situation into a win-win for both. You could even mentally request the energy to do whatever is in the highest good for all the parties involved.

Protection Shields

Bubbles and shields are extremely popular because they require very little work. However, their scope is limited and they can fail when one is placed in extremely trying situations.

Simple shields are merely used to stop energy, so their effect is the most limited. The advantage is that they are the easiest to create, and can be useful if we suddenly feel the need for protection. To make a simple shield, imagine yourself completely enveloped in a color that feels right for you. You can also shield others with their permission, and also objects such as homes and vehicles. Shields wear off after about 12 hours so they will need to be reapplied if needed.

Shields could be in the shape of a bubble, pyramid or cloak. Choose the one that you resonate with the most.

They can also be imagined in different colors, and every color has a different impact.

White light, the most popular one, protects the physical body against physical attack and crimes. It also invokes additional angels.

Pink light is the color of love and shields you against negativity.

Green light helps with physical healing and is wonderful to send to a person who is recovering from an injury or illness.

Purple light is for psychic protection and shields against psychic attack and entities.

Golden light offers all round protection, including grounding.

If you are feeling too vulnerable, you could also imagine yourself surrounded by a lightweight **lead** shield, protecting you from everything.

You can also pick up to three colors and layer them on top of each other for deeper protection.

Programmed Shields

Mirror Shield: Imagine a shield mirroring and reflecting back everything sent your way. The disadvantage is that this may not be too great for relationships as it reflects all the negativity back to the others in the room, and people might perceive negativity where there is none. Also, returning the negativity back to the sender sometimes creates a back-and-forth of energy, and might worsen the amount of negativity you are exposed to, should you forget to create a shield some time.

Absorb Shield: This takes care of the above-mentioned problem by simply absorbing the negativity being sent your way. You could imagine a thick, spongy layer around you, in violet if you want to transmute the energy being sent your way, or in red if you want to ground it. You could program this shield to absorb the negativity created not only by others, but also by yourself.

Fire Shield: The fire shield takes this a step further. Imagine yourself inside a ball of fire. Note that it is not a sphere of fire, it is more like a bubble – there is empty space inside, where you are located. You can request the fire to absorb and transmute all negativity coming towards it from inside as well as outside.

Shield of Invisibility: No, this does not make you disappear. It does make your aura invisible.

This is useful if it is you that is prone to feeling negative emotions towards someone else. Many times, light-workers tend to find it difficult around 'normal' people and get uncomfortable if they have to forcibly spend time with 'unconscious' people. If you are going to meet someone who you think doesn't like you, it is not their dislike of you that causes problems, but the energy you put out even before you meet them, resisting the meeting.

When we put out negativity, it comes back to us one way or another. To combat this, we can simply use the invisibility shield to protect others from our negativity, and to prevent related consequences. We can later request Reiki to heal our emotions when we practice our self-healing. This can also be used by healers who are feeling sympathetic towards a client, or by anyone experiencing fear while sensing a presence or during an attack.

To make this shield, imagine a transparent bubble around you and draw the clock-wise Cho-Ku-Rei on all four sides, and top and bottom. You could repeat the drawing of the symbols once more if required. If you don't practice Reiki or have only done level 1, you could imagine a cloak or shield which makes you invisible.

Creating a Psychic Shield

Here are the steps in detail, to create a shield.

- Decide which shield you want to create. If it is a mild situation, you want to create a simple shield. If you don't feel very strong and the attack is intense, it is easier to create a mirror or invisibility shield. Absorb shields are better when you are creating it in advance before going out to meet a group of people. If it is a strong attack but you are able to gather some strength, make a fire shield.
- Hara-center yourself. Focus your energy in the space just below your navel. If you are feeling ungrounded or unstable, imagine energy flowing in from the earth through your legs as you breathe in, and flowing back to the earth as you breathe out. Do this until you feel stable.
- Draw energy from the universe using your preferred method of healing.
- Now set the intention and create the shield in your preferred shape and color. Request the shield to do what you want it to do, for example reflect back all negativity.
- Shell it. Imagine the shield developing a hard shell and becoming impenetrable. Draw your favorite symbols on all sides if you like.

Removing the Shield

While most shields fade in about 12 to 24 hours, wearing shields take up your energy. The stronger the shield, the faster you are likely to feel tired. Many people also find that wearing shields at night can affect the quality of their sleep. For this reason it is a good idea to remove the shield when you have no more use for it.

To remove the shield, simply intend that its work is done. Thank it for its role, and visualize it disappearing or fading away and going back to the light.

Why Shields are Not Always Enough

There are many reasons why shields might not seem to work too well for you. For starters, they are based in the idea of separation, and not all, but many use them in fear. When we create shields out of fear of being hurt by another we are reinforcing our ideas of separation, which is nothing but the ego. Separation from another being also creates a separation from the universe, which often takes away divine grace as well.

Also, many healers tend to program their shields to let in only positive energies and keep all negative energies at bay. While this sounds wonderful, we forget that the basic nature of our universe is duality. When we swing too much towards one end, we will eventually swing towards the other like a pendulum. Too much positive energy is just as dangerous as too much negative energy. Like yin and yang, the key is in balance.

The world is like a mirror and only reflects your own reality back to you. So if you are facing too much negativity from the world while believing that you are yourself such a positive person, you need some dedicated shadow-work to come face to face with and integrate your own darkness.

Lastly, when we focus on the negativity of others, we forget that we are negative too. A shield can protect you from the negativity that others might send your way. But if someone triggers anger within you, that is still your mess to deal with, unless you have programed your shield to absorb your own negativity too.

Fire Cleanses

Fire almost always offers the most powerful cleansing. It is the only element that can easily transform matter into energy and thus connects both dimensions. The following solutions can be used to cleanse one's aura as well as one's living space.

In both processes given below, make sure that the bowl is placed on a surface, which will not catch fire or be damaged with the heat. Avoid doing this near curtains or books, and be careful with your clothes.

If possible, it is wonderful to have every family member participate in these ceremonies. If they all hold a strong intention to clear out old and unwanted energies, the process becomes much more powerful. If someone is affected by an entity, they are usually resistant to this process and might not want to participate, in which case coax them with love. Sometimes the entities also create difficulties in procuring the materials or by creating distractions that prevent you from performing these ceremonies, and in such a case the extra effort will be worth it.

The best place to perform these ceremonies is on the lowest floor and in the north, east or north-east corner of the house, as energies flow from east to west, north to south and down to up. It is a good idea to open windows to assist old energy in leaving the home.

CAUTION: Fire is great for burning away your impurities but it is also capable of burning much more than that. We advise you to exercise extreme caution while performing fire rituals.

Smudging

Smudging is a native American practice of clearing energies and involves the use of tobacco, cedar, sweet grass, juniper, pine needles, deer's tongue, pinion, cypress, and the most popular of them all, sage. If you want to make your own bundle, just bundle the twigs and tie it, and then let it hang upside down in cool, dark space until it is completely dried out.

Light your sage bundle on an Abalone shell if you have one, or a clay bowl. Light it with a match, gently blow out the flame and let the material continue to smolder. Take it around the house, starting in the East corner of your house and moving clockwise.

To smudge one's aura, once the bundle begins to smoke, start by holding the shell or bowl near the feet of the person, slowly moving upwards to the head, covering the whole body. Encircle the head three times and then repeat the same thing at the back. If you are doing this for yourself, skip the encircling of the head and only do as much of the back as is comfortably possible.

A Simple Fire

Simply making a fire and looking deeply into the flames as it burns, purifies the aura. When the fire is created with specific woods, the healing effect is deeper. The use of ghee also deepens the effect and adds Goddess energies to the ritual.

What you will need:

- A medium sized heat-proof vessel
- Some twigs or small pieces of wood. Wood from the trees which ooze white fluid when cut (the Ficus family) are the best for cleansing energies. Cow dung may also be used as it has very healing properties.
- If it is available, ghee (clarified butter)
- Camphor, if available
- Matches
- A lid you might want to use to put out the fire if it goes out of control

The process:

- Arrange the twigs in the vessel and place the camphor at the bottom.
- Light the camphor and let the twigs catch fire.
- If you are using ghee, you might add a few drops every few minutes to help with the burning.
- After the fire is extinguished, you may pour just a few drops of ghee on the ashes to increase the amount of smoke. This smoke is purifying and can be allowed to spread throughout the house. Of course, you can only do this if you do not have fire alarms.

Epsom Salt Fire

If you want to avoid smoke, this is a great option.

What you will need:

- A heat-safe bowl or an old coffee mug
- Rubbing alcohol or surgical spirits
- Epsom salts (sea salts could also be used)
- Matches

- A lid you might want to use to put out the fire if it goes out of control

The process:

- Place ¼ cup of Epsom salts into your heat-safe bowl and preferably place it on a large ceramic or steel plate.
- Gently pour rubbing alcohol onto the salts until it is just damp, not soaking wet. About 2 tablespoons should be enough. Take care not to accidentally drop the alcohol on your hands or clothes.
- You may invoke your favorite deities, guides, angels, ancestors, or God and request them for assistance.
- Light a match and touch it to the mixture. It will light up immediately. If the flame is too high, extinguish the fire by covering the bowl with the lid, add a little more salt and light again.
- Imagine this blue flame burning up all the dark, stagnant and heavy energies in the house and transmuting them into light.
- If you like, you can now lift the plate carefully and walk around the house to each room.
- After the ritual is over, discard the salts after they cool by flushing them down the toilet.

Fire Circle

To make a fire circle light eight lamps or candles and place them in a wide circle, leaving enough space for you to sit comfortably inside. If it feels right you may also place a flower next to each candle; this will soften the effect of the fire on your own body and reduce the drying effect it tends to have. If you like using crystals, place cleansed and charged Carnelian, Fire Agate or Amber alongside each candle to strengthen the lower two chakras, as fire can be un-grounding.

Before you enter the circle, ensure that you are not wearing inflammable or loose, flowing clothes. Take care that you are not too close to the fire. Also, make sure that the candles or lamps are placed on fire-proof surfaces and that there are no curtains or papers nearby. This process works best in the dark, so switch off the lights before you begin.

Once you are comfortably settled within the circle, close your eyes and imagine that the fire is burning away all the impurities in your aura. You will slowly start to feel a crisp, light feeling where dull energies start to clear out. Once your aura fairly clears up, imagine that you are breathing in fire. It enters through your nose and spreads through the energy channels in your body to every corner, burning away every impurity. Try not to be particularly attached to burning away a specific emotion. Instead, let the fire even burn away the desire to tackle a specific problem. Let every block, every impurity burn away.

If this was merely for routine cleansing or a minor attack, you can put out the candles once the process is over. If you were doing this to clear out major or repetitive attacks, you can end this process by creating the fire shield.

Fire can dry up your body so if this is overdone, there might be slight itching in the eyes or dryness of the skin. Too much fire in the body over time can also cause acne and breakouts. You might want to follow this ritual up with gentle oil massages and / or eating nourishing foods containing good fats, like porridges, congee, *khichdi* (lentil and rice porridge) with ghee, etc.

Cleansing Spaces

The place we live in, directly reflects the energy we carry. However, since the walls absorb our energy, the house may still be weighed down even after you have healed. It is therefore a good idea to cleanse your living spaces regularly, especially after someone has been ill, or if the family has gone through a difficult time.

Clear out the mess. Clutter brings in messy energies. To start clearing out your 'space', you have to start by clearing out the things. Get rid of things you haven't used for a while, because junk brings in a persistent dull, stagnant energy.

Visualization/ Flooding. Imagine a flood of loving energy coming in through the ceiling and filling up the whole space, taking all unwanted energies out of the window. Many people tend to request Reiki to fill the space with positive energy, but I've seen this to remain stable only about twelve hours as positive and negative are part of duality and they eventually replace the other. Instead, request Reiki to create balance in the house. If there isn't much disturbance in the form of visitors or negative emotions in the house, this balanced energy can remain stable for up to four days.

Bells/ Singing Bowls. Walk around your house ringing a bell or using a singing bowl to cleanse your space. This, along with flooding is a great option to cleanse external spaces when you want to conduct a workshop, or move in to a house for a short vacation as they are quick, easy, and in case of bells or small singing bowls, easy to carry.

Incense. Using incense regularly gently clears the energy of your house. Sandalwood, Jasmine, Sunflower and High John are helpful for purification and protection. You can light these on a daily basis to raise the vibration in your home.

House Clearing Room Sprays. You can purchase these online but it is best to make your own. They are made with essential oils and not synthetic fragrances, as essential oils carry the vibration from the specific flower. Sage, lavender, frankincense, patchouli, cedar and myrrh are good choices.

To make your own spray, fill three-fourths of a glass bottle with spring or filtered water and add the following items:

- 4 to 8 drops of sage essential oil
- 2 to 4 drops of any other essential oil of your choice
- a pinch of rock salt or sea salt
- You could also add fresh sage or holy basil leaf and a few white rose petals into the bottle.
- Add a teaspoon of alcohol if you want to preserve the spray.
- You could add a small crystal inside or place a few large crystals around the bottle to charge it. Black Obsidian is a great choice for cleansing, Rose Quartz for charging the space with love.

You could also charge it by leaving it overnight under the full moon. And lastly, don't forget to charge your spray with Reiki!

Now simply go around the house and spray it towards the ceiling in all corners of every room.

Rock Salt and Candles. This is an easy ritual to perform whenever you need to cleanse a space, and is a must-do whenever you move in to a new house, preferably on the first few nights. Place rock salt in little bowls in the center of every room, or all four corners of a room if you're trying to cleanse just one room. Next to the salt, place lamps or little candles. Take care to ensure that there is no inflammable material near the candle. Leave this overnight to absorb all negative energy, and then clean it out in the morning, flushing the salts.

Fire and smoke. Using sage, allow smoke to clear out the energies. Burning camphor is also a good idea because it brings a very clean, crisp energy in. If you have been hearing sounds, creaks, thuds or footsteps, use one of the fire rituals listed above.

Heal your house. Walk around the house and mentally draw the symbols on every wall. Everything has life, and if the house has picked up your pain, then this pain needs healing too. As you stand in front of every wall, allow yourself to feel love and compassion towards that wall, and request it to release all the pain it is holding.

This may be a little hard in the beginning if you've thought of inanimate objects as dead and lifeless, but once you can bring yourself to connect with them and see their pain, you will be able to bring in the same attitude that you would have if you were healing a sick person. And when that happens this is the most effective.

I recommend drawing all the symbols as the distant healing symbol will connect to that moment in time when the wall absorbed the pain, the emotional healing symbol will heal it, and the power symbol seals the new energies in.

In every room, once you are done healing all the walls, also heal the space inside. Draw the symbols mentally in the center of the room and request Reiki to clear out the space and fill it with love and light.

At the end of the healing, heal the house as a whole, drawing the symbols mentally on the outside walls as well, and sealing the energy with the power symbol.

If you haven't been attuned to level 2, you can skip the symbols part, and just place your hands on the walls, requesting Reiki to cleanse and heal it. To clear out the space inside the room, you could either heal a glass of water with Reiki and sprinkle that around the room, or Reiki an air freshener and spray that around.

Karmic Healing

When one is faced with difficulties that don't make any sense, one is often prompted to ask where the root of such a problem might lie. In cases of serious psychic attacks that affect the life of a person for many years, the root is often in previous lives.

Many people who undergo intense suffering as a result of being subjected to psychic attack of black magic have an unpleasant past-life history where they have harmed others. Accessing these memories doesn't usually help more than some sort of consolation that there is a reason for what is going on.

When a whole family seems to attract the same kind of problems, it is a case of group karma. In such a case it is not required that every single family member participate in resolving the issue. Individuals who work at the solution will find that they are not affected anymore, even if the rest of the family is still suffering. Every single person who heals, also raises the vibration of the whole group and helps the others find a solution more easily, should they try to heal the problem.

What is Past Karma?

There are two types of karmic baggage that we bring with us from the past. One is the type where we have hurt others in some way, and this is coming back to haunt us. The other is where someone has hurt us, and we have refused to forgive, thereby carrying a conscious or subconscious desire to hurt the other, or see the other 'learn a lesson'.

While the first type might be impacting our present, the second type more likely impacts our future.

How Does Karma Work?

Karma is nothing but attachment, and the circumstances around it propagate a continuation of this attachment. For instance, if a person A loves some object, say a vintage pot, and person B breaks this pot in a fit of anger, karma is created. Not so much due to the breakage of the item, but because of the person's attachment to it. Person A now wants to teach the other a lesson. So eventually, they exchange roles, and just for the sake of the example, let us assume that again, a pot is broken – this time by person A. Now person B wants to teach A a lesson, and the story continues.

These things get further complicated when we want to punish ourselves. When we are very attached to our sense of right and wrong, we not only want others to be punished, but we are also much harsher on ourselves. At the time of death, many of us review our mistakes and decide to punish ourselves. The healing of this aspect is of prime importance with regards to healing ones past lives.

Will this Make my Problems Go Away?

People very commonly mistake karma for problems. They are not the same thing. Every action has a set consequence, and nothing can change that. For example, if one is trying to come to the USA from Australia, there is going to be an ocean to cross. It is absolutely impossible to drive all the way. Every journey has its share of obstacles, and if anything, these obstacles only help us grow, evolve and mature. Taking away our problems will take away our potential to grow.

Karma does not bring problems. It brings suffering. Suffering distracts, and prevents us from seeing clearly and finding an easy solution. Healing your past karma may or may not clear your problem entirely, but it will help you come to terms with what is going on, and deal with it the best you possibly can.

How can I let it go?

Karma is nothing but a continuation of attachment. Unless we let go of our own attachments – either attachments to certain people or objects or the attachment to the idea of seeing someone else learn a lesson and improve, the karma cannot be completely cleared.

The Process

Bringing oneself in complete acceptance of the present situation along with the emotions that are being triggered is the most effective way to dissolve all karma. However this is not always easy, so here's a process that you can follow to reduce your karmic impact on a difficult current situation.

Deepen your Insight: The first step would be to obtain a deeper insight into what impact the situation is having on us. Writing helps tremendously with this process, and I suggest spending some time writing for a few days, about what your feelings about your current situation are. Write *only* about your own feelings, and not about what others should or should not be doing. As you write about your feelings, ask yourself if there is another emotion hiding underneath what you are feeling. For example, one might be angry at first, but on further investigation, might realize that it was actually humiliation or helplessness that was being masked by the anger. A little time spent in investigation everyday can take you very deep and greatly enhance your healing.

Embrace your Feelings: Once you are clear what feelings this situation invokes, the next step is relaxing in these feelings. It is when we try to escape feeling a certain way that we get deeper into trouble. So, although it may sound counter intuitive, think about your current situation, feel the way it makes you feel, and allow this to happen. I would suggest not trying to rush through the process – it may take you a few days of practice to be able to relax into the feeling. By this, I mean that you will be comfortable with the feelings that come up, without a desire to make the feeling go away by doing or saying something to somebody.

You could also combine this process with your self-healing, allowing the feeling to come up just before you begin, and then going through your Reiki self-healing, so that Reiki can help with your process.

Dissolve the Past: Once you are comfortable in the feeling, it is time to heal the past. Bring your energy to your heart chakra, and request the universe / Reiki to

1)   Connect you with all events that are contributing to the current situation in your life
2)   Heal all emotions associated with these situations and people
3)   And to help to retain your focus in your heart, so that you can view everything through the perspective of love, faith and compassion
4)   If other people are also involved in your situation, imagine them all sitting in front of you and flood them with love and energy

5) Sit quietly for some time, allowing your body to settle into the new energies.

The deepest healing does not occur in a sudden burst, but is the result of continuous dedication. Done over a period of time, this process will help you release much of the karma that is holding you back in life.

Strengthening Your Aura

The strengthening of the aura is very important not just during the healing process but also after. If one is prone to psychic attacks these processes go a long way in minimizing or even eliminating them.

Grounding

One of the most profound aspects of nature is its stillness. Stillness is also one of the primary things humanity has sacrificed at the altar of modern living. With the population exploding, we are either surrounded by external noise – voices, vehicles, planes flying overhead – or internal noise – thought pollution.

The current world is always moving, always growing, leaving no space or tolerance for silence. Or stillness. It is a very heavy price to pay.

Continuous movement, both of the body and the mind, send the energy shooting upwards. It is like we're constantly reaching out for the skies, with no eye on the ground. If one ever studies a tree, one knows that a tree with longer, stronger roots is far better equipped to survive. It will withstand the heaviest storms, because it is deeply rooted, being held securely in the womb of the earth. Storms might come and rip away its branches, but it will sprout forth with vigor again, as if nothing were ever wrong.

In contrast, a tree that has focused all of its energies in flowering or yielding fruits while neglecting the development of its roots, will not only have paler flowers, smaller fruits, but also no stability in the face of a storm. Unfortunately, this is a metaphor for what most of us look like today.

Nature always takes time to go inwards, to focus on what is really important. Everything fluctuates, nothing is ever constant. Leaves fall, trees look nearly dead and then spring back to life. Growth is seldom expected a hundred percent of the time, it comes in waves instead. We've forgotten this basic fact. The society needs to see continuous growth, things can never slow down. And we expect the same from the mind.

We spend so much time focusing on getting what we want, that we forget completely to look at what we need. The lower chakras are deprived, shrunken and shriveled for want of nourishment, but neither our minds nor our lifestyles support this. The lack of direct contact with nature, the continuous stimulation of the senses through over-seasoned junk foods, video games, TV shows, the literal un-grounding through planes and high speed trains all push our energies further upwards. There is almost nothing to bring us back down.

Psychic attacks only happen to people who have very poor or negligible grounding. Unfortunately, poor grounding is almost a universal problem today, which means not being under psychic attack is more often a matter of good luck than anything else.

Luckily, grounding is actually not too hard, but it does take a little dedication and effort. Here are a few simple ways of getting grounded.

Connect with Nature

Most of the times when people spend time in nature, they are again moving. Trekking, climbing, always with a goal and somewhere else to be. This takes away the biggest advantage of spending time in nature. To benefit from nature the most, one needs to be in one place as much as possible, with slow, casual walking. Do nothing. As mentioned earlier, hugging a tree backwards and walking barefoot on grass with the intention of reconnecting with the earth are also quick, helpful exercises.

Exercise

Today's fast-paced calorie-burning exercise disconnects us with our bodies. Most even want music to help them ignore the pain and push themselves beyond healthy limits. Physical activities like yoga, tai chi, qi gong help with grounding as long as they are done slowly, with awareness and without distractions like music. It has to be done with the objective of coming back to the body as deeply as possible, and not with the objective of 'feeling peaceful'.

For a quick-fix, doing the tree pose (*vrikshasana*) holding for about 3 minutes on each side is very effective in bringing instant stability. To prevent losing your balance, stare at a spot in front of you. It is even more effective when performed while looking at the rising sun.

Massage

A good massage using the right oils can nourish both the root and the sacral chakras. One needn't even go to a spa; simply massaging oils like mustard oil, Ayurvedic Vata massage oils or oils with herbs or essences like patchouli on a daily basis just before bedtime or before bath can help to ground very effectively. For best results, it is advisable to use lentil or herbal powders to wash the body, as soaps dry the skin and also reduce grounding.

The Right Foods

Highly processed foods are far removed from the earth and reduce our grounding. Foods that grow below the earth like carrots, potatoes, parsnips, beets, radishes, onions and garlic, all help soothe the root chakra. The color of the root chakra is red, so all red fruits and vegetables help with grounding too.

Color Therapy

Avoiding upper chakra colors like blue, violet and white on the lower half of your body may be a good idea for a while as you try to re-establish your grounding. Reds, browns and blacks are great colors to support the root chakra. You might also want to check the color of your carpets – earthy colors like green, red and browns ground you, while colors of the sky will leave your body confused and your aura unstable, as the subconscious perceives sky and water everywhere, neither of which bring stability. Having a picture of a mountain or a tree facing you where you spend the most of your time can also help.

Meditation for Grounding

Many decades ago, before we entered the information age, the lower chakras were stable as people were strongly connected to the earth and to their local surroundings. Many even lived in harmony with nature. For such people, spiritual evolution meant moving upwards. We still follow the same methods for spiritual evolution, but the circumstances have completely changed. Meditation on the root chakra is far more powerful than meditating on the very popular third eye. It may not give you the vision and clairvoyance the third eye can, but it will also spare you the resulting side effects, the alienation from the outer world, feeling of never belonging anywhere, and lack of energy. It will instead, bring you a stable and calmer mind, a more relaxed and stronger body, much better energy levels, an immunity from boredom and more important than anything else, psychic protection.

There are various ways to improve grounding through meditation.

Meditating on the Root Chakra

Meditating on the symbol:

• You could paste the root chakra symbol in various places around your room or house to remind you to ground yourself. To meditate, focus on the symbol of the root chakra.

• Gently resist blinking. Do not force it, but consciously reduce the frequency of blinking.

• When your eyes get tired, let them close on their own. Retain the picture of the root chakra in your mind.

• You can chant the root chakra syllable *'lam'* (pronounced *lung)* a few times if it feels right for you.

• If you feel distracted or the mind wanders, you could open your eyes, focus on the symbol and repeat.

Meditating on the root chakra:

• Sit on the floor if you can, or on a chair. Be comfortable, spine erect without straining. Close your eyes.

• Imagine a red ball of fire at the tip of your tailbone.

- This ball of fire slowly expands as you breathe in, and slightly contracts as you breathe out, resonating with your breath.
- When it feels right, imagine the ball expanding a little more than last time with every inhalation.

Visualization

- Sit on the floor if you can, or on a chair. Be comfortable, spine erect without straining. Close your eyes.
- Visualize your auric field as a sphere enveloping your whole body. If you see any colors naturally it is great, otherwise you may imagine it to be transparent or red.
- Imagine this slowly changing shape, becoming a triangle. Feel all the energy shifting to the ground.
- Retain this shape in your mind for as long as possible.

Connecting with the Earth

- Sit on the floor if you can, or on a chair. If possible, this meditation is best done outdoors or under a tree. Be comfortable, spine erect without straining. Close your eyes.
- As you breathe out, imagine your energy flowing down through your tailbone and into the earth, forming roots.
- When you breathe in, imagine that you are receiving nourishment from mother earth, and this energy is flowing in through your tailbone and nourishing your whole body.
- This can also be done in the tree pose, but with the eyes open as closing your eyes will cause you to lose balance.

Aromatherapy

Smell is the primary sense related to the root chakra. Synthetic perfume smells therefore very quickly affect the root chakra and destabilize it. Using essential oils however, can be effective for grounding. Fragrances like patchouli, sandalwood, cedar wood, myrrh and frankincense are wonderful for this purpose.

Integrating the Shadow

From a very young age, we are subjected to the ideas of good and bad. Good is made out to be worthy of our attention while bad is presented as despicable. Our fairytales talk about perfectly good heroes who always win and perfectly bad monsters who always die. We're taught to like the light and dislike the shadows.

We're seldom taught that they cannot exist without the other. That is where the problem begins.

As young children, our biggest fear related to survival is abandonment. To ensure that our parents don't lose interest in us and leave us in the wild, we are subconsciously programed to develop the qualities that they reward and suppress the qualities that they reject. Added to the education about good and bad and the rejection of all that is bad, this forms a life-long pattern of rejecting everything in ourselves that we find unacceptable.

When we live in denial, not only is it impossible to improve in those areas, but we also open ourselves to manipulation. Someone who is identified with being a 'kind' person for instance, can be used by manipulating them into a situation where they would need to be unkind to get out.

The idea of integrating the shadow is extremely scary to many. Questions like 'but if I accept my anger, what if I end up hurting somebody?' are common. Acceptance is not the same as translating into action. There is a middle path between expression and suppression –and that is what shadow-work is all about.

Our shadow can be compared with a normal shadow. Let us take our house for example. There are areas which are well lit, and there are areas which are hidden in shadows. If we refused to acknowledge the existence of the areas which were shadowed, would that really change anything? They would still continue to exist. However, since we deny their existence, we would never be able to clean them, and eventually they would become festering spots of negativity, foul, stinking and spreading disease. This is why shadow-work is necessary. It is not the encouragement of darkness, simply the acceptance of it and eventually learning to make the most of it. After all, the shadows don't always hide only the bad stuff!

Finding the Shadow

The first pre-requisite in working with the shadow is brutal honesty with the self. Shadows are aspects of us that we hate, are ashamed of, and want to pretend doesn't exist. The mind will do anything to continue pretending that these aspects don't exist and it is easy to get tricked into this if we aren't honest enough with ourselves.

Finding the shadow is actually quite easy. Absolutely anything that triggers a strong reaction within us is the shadow. This may be good or bad. For example, if someone is repeatedly addicted to people who praise them, it feels good but is an indicator of a low self-esteem and an incapacity to look at the best within people (which is the aspect they are representing). On the other hand, if someone gets terribly ticked off with every obese person, it is an indication of complete lack of acceptance of the fat or curves in his or her own body.

It is OK to have a Shadow

Since we are taught from a young age to reject the shadow, coming face to face with it causes us stress. This shows up in the body at related locations and prevents free flow of energy in the body, causing disease. Energetically it creates gaps in our field which can be utilized by entities.

Before we begin shadow-work, we have to repeat to ourselves that it is perfectly fine to be 'bad'. This does not mean it is alright to hurt someone else or to do something bad. It does mean that it is ok to have feelings we normally judge as bad. For example, it is not OK to shout at someone and beat them up. However, it is perfectly fine to *feel* angry.

Unfortunately, we confuse feeling with expressing. They are completely different and don't have to be related at all. Just like if you placed your hand on a hot stove you would experience pain, when you encounter situations in life you feel things emotionally. What you feel is a natural reaction of your system and must not be judged. Actions are another matter. Interestingly, when we learn to accept our feelings as natural we will find that we are in a much better position to act sensibly even when our feelings run amok.

Working with the Shadow

To begin working with the shadow, we must begin to see the problems we have with others as a reflection of our own inner reality. As we are programmed to resist anything unpleasant, it is a natural reaction to want the feeling to go away. We have to learn to ignore this reaction and learn to 'settle' into the feeling, slowly inching towards accepting it. The process in itself is easy, but it needs dedication and honesty to make it effective and powerful.

Whenever you experience an intense feeling whether good or bad, sit with your spine comfortably erect (or lie down) and do the following.

- Start with reminding yourself that no matter how justified your feelings seem, they are still *your* feelings and are based on a partial perception of reality.
- Become aware of the resistance towards these emotions.
- Ignore the thoughts and the stories that come up. Do not listen to the mind, keep your focus on the feelings. Feelings can be described in one word – angry, hurt, frustrated, guilty, ashamed, ecstatic, etc. It is not about the other person, it is about you.
- While becoming deeply aware of the feelings, simultaneously become aware of your breath. Feel it as deeply in your body as possible, preferably in the chest and belly.
- It is perfectly fine to feel this pain/ joy. Allow yourself to feel it, no matter how uncomfortable it is. Do not pay attention to any thoughts.
- Now bring your attention to your entire body. Become aware of any sensations in your body. It could

be tightness, heat, cold, burning, a sinking feeling, tingling, etc. If this part naturally relaxes when you become aware of it that is ok, but do not force this part of your body to relax. Merely become aware of the sensation and watch it.

• If this becomes too intense or hard to handle, go back to watching your breath.

• You may end this exercise when you feel that you have totally relaxed into the situation. i.e., even if there is stress, you are not resisting the stress; if there is pain, you are not resisting the pain.

Life Wants You to Integrate

Negative emotions are provided to us by nature for protection and survival, and are naturally much more intense than positive emotions whose only real purpose is to help us reproduce. When we reject our darkness, we also reject with it our inner power, because it is only in the acceptance of our negativity that we can truly access our own power.

Our higher-self knows this, and craves for this integration so that we can be whole again. It repeatedly presents our shadow sides through other people in our lives. For example, a person who has rejected his or her anger will almost never get angry but will repeatedly come across people who are extremely angry. As we practice more and more awareness, we can start to integrate everything that life mirrors back to us, moving one step at a time towards a more grounded, powerful and yet peaceful personality.

Reclaim your Inner Power

Integrating the shadow leads to a natural integration of inner power but since it is a critical issue for many, I felt it merited a section for itself. Until the shadow is integrated, it is very hard for us to be able to use our negative emotions in the right way, and we have a strong tendency to respond to perceived threats through fight or flight responses – submissiveness or aggression.

It is a beautiful thing to watch balanced, assertive people handle difficult life situations. While aggressive people seem powerful to most, that is not really the case. The aggression is just a mask to hide the lack of power they are experiencing.

So, both aggressive as well as submissive people benefit tremendously by taking their power back. But what does this mean?

Submissive: Those who don't know how to say 'no'. These people wind up doing a whole lot of things that they don't want to do. Those who are very submissive will end up taking on way more than they can handle, which means they will end up letting a lot of people down. They then also tend to be very apologetic, saying and feeling sorry very frequently. They tend to take the blame for everything.

Example for a submissive response: "I'm so sorry, it's just not possible for me to do this. I'm so stuck with my job, my boss really overloads me and I come home so tired, I don't know what to do."

Aggressive: These people are the opposite, saying no a bit too forcefully, having little regard for others' feelings or personal space. They often encourage others to do things for them through flattery or manipulation. They have a tendency to blame others for everything that goes wrong.

Example for an aggressive response: "Why should I do this? Don't I have anything better to do?"

Assertive: While there may be some people who are naturally assertive, assertion is usually a learned behavior, or develops as a result of healing personal anger and power issues. These people are able to clearly state their difficulty/ needs without encroaching on the personal space of others.

Example for assertive response: "I can't do this right now because I'm tied up with something else at the moment. Does tomorrow work?"

There are articles that help you deal with this from the level of the mind, to help you go from being submissive or aggressive to being assertive. However, taking the energy approach heals this from the root cause, and assertive responses become much more genuine, and thereby more effective.

Work with the Solar Plexus and Thighs

If you seek any kind of healing, healing all the chakras on your body, both front and back, is very important.

Otherwise, the problems can just shift to another chakra temporarily. If you wish to resolve power issues, heal all the points every day. When you come to these specific points, you can do the following.

Step 1 (21 days): Heal the solar plexus as well as thighs, using all the symbols if you have learned the higher levels, with a desire to heal all power related issues. While you are healing your solar plexus, mentally request your body to prioritize healing your power related issues, and to bring up any hidden problems in this regard. It is wise to do this only when you have no other pressing issue to resolve, as it might lead to erratic behavior, mood swings, aches or fatigue.

You might need to continue just step 1 for 2-3 weeks to clear out suppressed issues. If you sense that the issues you are working with are really deep, do it for 3 months.

Step 2 (21 days): Visualize the power symbol within the solar plexus, and hold this image in a meditative space for as long as is comfortable. The effect of this will be temporary if the previous step is not complete. Do this only after step 1 is over.

Closing Remarks

Our societal and parental conditioning usually leads us to believe that we are weak and need support from outside, through lovers/ spouses, children, a house, financial stability, etc. There are thousands of teachers and masters telling you that it is possible to live a perfect life and that you can get all of these if you just follow what is written in their book, or said in their video, or taught in their workshop.

This is the paradox of the current idea of spirituality – when people get tired of chasing after money, love and power through traditional means, today they turn to 'spiritual tools'. These 'spiritual' tools make great promises, but they leave us devoid of one major thing – the lesson that we are complete in ourselves.

Happiness does not lie in that brand new Ferrari, or that 6-bedroom Beverly Hills house, or that model wife/ industrialist husband and children that study in International schools and ace every subject. Happiness is a choice that we have to train ourselves to make. Many times things fall into place by themselves when this happens. Even if it doesn't, it doesn't matter so much because we're happy nevertheless.

It is highly essential to learn this one lesson, as this is the strongest protection against psychic attack. When we are highly invested in a particular outcome from life, it leaves a gaping void within us. This void will then be filled with food, partying, internet and entities. If instead, we embrace our life as it is and work wholeheartedly on making the most of it, we grow into strong, healthy individuals.

It Isn't Always Psychic Attack

While I come across a lot of people who are under psychic attack and have no idea, or refuse to believe it, I also come across people who are not under psychic attack but are running pillar to post to find a solution. Sometimes, life just doesn't bring us what we want. Instead of surrendering to this fact, if we keep pushing in a direction where we feel we are justified in our demands, whether that be a promotion or a marriage or a child, the incessant failures might lead us to believe that something is psychically wrong. What is wrong is that we're failing to get the message the life is trying to teach us – that there may be a completely different story planned out for us.

At other times I have found that some people suddenly come face to face with their shadow and the shadow is so intense that it almost has a life of its own. Simply shadow-work is enough in this case, although it might take some time for complete healing.

Become the Light

All psychic, emotional and physical vulnerabilities are places within ourselves where we are identified with the wounds we're carrying from our past.

If we set about healing those wounds through the many, many tools available - like Reiki, hypnotherapy, meditation, etc. - we will eventually dissolve these vulnerabilities and all the tools mentioned in this book will be unnecessary.

We need to stop chasing to 'find the right technique/ teacher/ crystal', because the real solution does not lie outside. We need to seek less to 'surround ourselves with white light' and more to *become* that light, learning to identify not with thoughts and emotions but the pure consciousness that animates them. When you are completely grounded within yourself and in complete surrender to the present moment, no psychic attack or entity can affect you.

About the Author

Having learned Meditation as a child, **Ashwita Goel** *incorporated Reiki into her life during her early teens. After a decade of witnessing the magic Reiki, she felt compelled to take up Reiki professionally, and ended her corporate career in 2007, taking up Reiki full-time. She eventually incorporated EFT, hypnotherapy and past life therapy into her work. Apart from her healing work, she teaches Reiki and meditation. Her other book* **'Healing Through Reiki'** *is available on Amazon.*

You can connect with Ashwita through Facebook https://www.facebook.com/Reiki.Bangalore, *her website* http://www.reiki-bangalore.com/ *or visit her blog* http://www.ashwita.com/zen/.

54276420R00057

Made in the USA
San Bernardino, CA
12 October 2017